Battle of the Bands

Using Data and Graphs

Consultants

Pamela Dase, M.A.Ed.
National Board Certified Teacher

Barbara Talley, M.S.
Texas A&M University

Publishing Credits

Dona Herweck Rice, *Editor-in-Chief*
Robin Erickson, *Production Director*
Lee Aucoin, *Creative Director*
Timothy J. Bradley, *Illustration Manager*
Sara Johnson, M.S.Ed., *Senior Editor*
Aubrie Nielsen, M.S.Ed., *Associate Education Editor*
Jennifer Kim, M.A.Ed., *Associate Education Editor*
Neri Garcia, *Senior Designer*
Stephanie Reid, *Photo Editor*
Rachelle Cracchiolo, M.S.Ed., *Publisher*

Image Credits

Cover Jacetan/Dreamstime; p.1 Jacetan/Dreamstime; p.4 (top) RoxyFer/Shutterstock, (bottom) Brian Chase/Shutterstock; p.5 (top) criben/Shutterstock, (bottom) photobank.kiev.ua/Shutterstock; p.6 (left) Ronald Sumners/Shutterstock, (right) Lisa F. Young/Shutterstock, (inset) Nicemonkey/ Shutterstock; p.8–9 EschCollection/Getty Images; p.9 (left) Photodisc/Photo Library, (right) Milosz Aniol/Shutterstock; p.10 David Gilder/Shutterstock; p.11 (left) Keith Publicover/ Shutterstock, (right) Petr Malyshev/Shutterstock; p.12 (left) Tea/Dreamstime.com, (right) wellphoto/Shutterstock, (inset) Coprid/Shutterstock; p.13 (left) Ronald Sumners/Shutterstock, (right) morchella/Shutterstock; p.14 (left) Tim Bradley, (center) Tim Bradley, (right) Ruslan Ivantsov/Shutterstock; p.16–17 Benis Arapovic/Shutterstock; p.17 Inti St Clair/Photo Library; p.18 (top) rafalkrakowrafalkrakow/iStockphoto, (center) Sean Nel/Shutterstock, (bottom) Alexey Laputin/Shutterstock; p.18–19 Ben Dome/Nathanael Jones, PacificCoastNews; p.20 (top) webphotographeer/iStockphoto, (bottom) pjhpix/Shutterstock, (inset) dean bertoncelj/Shutterstock; p.20–21 Demonike/Dreamstime; p.22–23 RoxyFer/Shutterstock; p.23 BRIAN SNYDER/RTR/ Newscom; p.24 sjlocke/iStockphoto; p.25 Keith Publicover/Shutterstock; p.26 Oliver Gutfleisch; p.27 (top) BOB FILA KRT/Newscom, (center) miss_pj/iStockphoto, (bottom) corepics/ Shutterstock, (inset) GoodMood Photo/Shutterstock; p.28 GoodMood Photo/Shutterstock; All other images: Shutterstock

Teacher Created Materials

5301 Oceanus Drive
Huntington Beach, CA 92649-1030
http://www.tcmpub.com

ISBN 978-1-4333-3465-8

© 2012 Teacher Created Materials, Inc.

Table of Contents

JUL 2016

Music for a Good Cause 4

Planning the Show 6

Pre-Concert Details 12

Show Time! 18

A Successful Event 24

Problem-Solving Activity 28

Glossary 30

Index 31

Answer Key 32

Music for a Good Cause

The kids at school are really excited! People around town are excited, too. They are waiting for something that has been planned for weeks. Tonight is the Battle of the Bands event. Musicians from around the area are performing. The concert will be a competition to determine the most popular band.

Benefit Concerts

Typically the proceeds from concert ticket sales go to pay band members and to cover concert costs. Occasionally, a band or musician will agree to perform at a benefit concert. In that case, fans buy tickets but the proceeds go to a charitable organization or cause rather than to the band.

The best part of this event is that the money raised tonight will help tornado victims. A local town was struck by a strong tornado this year. The town was seriously damaged. Many people lost their homes. Even the high school was destroyed.

Many volunteers are trying to fix the damage caused by the tornado. Our town wanted to help. We decided to raise money with this community event.

Planning the Show

Bands that play different kinds of music have offered to participate. There will be rap, hip-hop, rock, pop, reggae (REG-ey), and country music. Some school bands will perform, too. Everyone wants this event to be a lot of fun.

A Battle of the Bands contest is always interesting for the audience. They can hear music that they might not listen to at home. A **diverse** (dih-VURS) line-up boosts ticket sales. The more tickets that are sold, the more money there will be to donate.

The bands are volunteering their time. They will not be paid for performing. They want as much money as possible to go to the tornado victims. That is why they agreed to a benefit concert.

A local event planner offered to **coordinate** the Battle of the Bands. To plan the event, she looked at the results of a survey of 550 students. The survey asked how many songs should be performed at the event. The results of the survey are displayed on the **histogram** below.

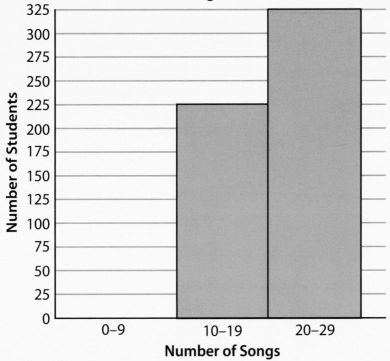

Number of Songs for the Concert

a. What **interval** did the event planner use to represent the number of songs on the histogram?

b. The first interval is 0–9 songs. How many people said they thought 0–9 songs should be included in the event?

c. Based on the survey results, how many songs do you think should be included in the program? Why?

The event planner is in charge of many behind-the-scenes details. She has worked with each band to give them information about the show.

The Battle of the Bands is taking place at the town's outdoor **amphitheater** (AMP-fuh-thee-uh-ter). The event planner is responsible for tickets, refreshments, parking, and souvenirs (soo-vuh-NEERZ). She puts someone in charge of each of these areas. She also works with a stage manager. That person is in charge of what happens onstage tonight. He will help with instruments, microphones, and speakers. He will also help get each band on and off the stage during the show.

Concert Venues

A **venue** (VEN-yoo) is a place where performances are held. Concerts can take place in all different sizes of venues.

Not Just for Concerts

Stage managers are found in all types of productions. Plays, ballets, and operas all require a stage manager.

LET'S EXPLORE MATH

This histogram shows the same data as the previous graph. The size of the intervals has been changed.

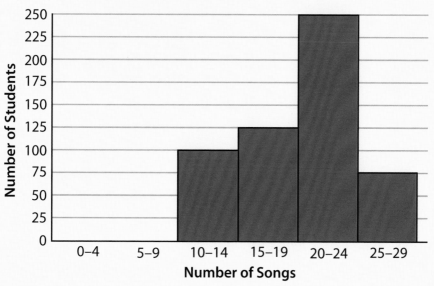

Number of Songs for the Concert

Number of Students (y-axis: 0, 25, 50, 75, 100, 125, 150, 175, 200, 225, 250)

Number of Songs (x-axis: 0–4, 5–9, 10–14, 15–19, 20–24, 25–29)

a. What interval did the event planner use for this histogram?

b. Using this graph, how many songs would you include in the program?

The Battle of the Bands schedule took some work. The event planner worked with the stage manager to figure out the order in which the bands should perform. Sometimes the equipment needed influences that decision. For example, perhaps several bands need a keyboard. It would work well to have those bands near each other on the schedule.

Booking Agents

When bands or musicians are famous and have a lot of fans, the event planner has to work closely with various booking agents. Booking agents are the people who arrange to use the stadiums or arenas where artists perform while on tour.

Aliah investigated the length of 20 different Battle of the Bands concerts. She found the following lengths of concerts in minutes: 95, 102, 117, 160, 100, 128, 122, 75, 130, 132, 113, 125, 112, 120, 155, 126, 121, 90, 145, 168.

a. What are the maximum and minimum lengths of concerts she found?

b. To graph this data, what would be a good interval for the number of minutes?

c. Make a histogram for the data.

d. Using your graph, what do you think would be a reasonable amount of time for the battle to last?

The schedule also helps the planner know how long the show will last. The owners of the amphitheater have a limit for how long the event can last. Also, the fans will not want to sit for too long. Having a schedule to follow will help the organizers keep the concert moving.

Pre-Concert Details

Many of the bands have never played for such a big crowd, so they are nervous about this event. They hope that people enjoy their performances.

When playing for a large crowd, musicians have to prepare for a performance in a different way. The bands have to get used to the size and layout of the stage. They have to know where to stand while they perform and how to "work the stage" for a good performance. They also have to know how to **amplify** (AM-pluh-fahy) their sound so that the quality of the music is good for the venue size. Special sound equipment may be needed. The stage manager works with sound technicians. They know how to make all of the instruments sound great.

mixing console

amplifiers

The Battle of the Bands has rented sound equipment from the same company for each of the last five years. The **line graphs** below show the costs over the years. A line graph is a graph that shows change over time.

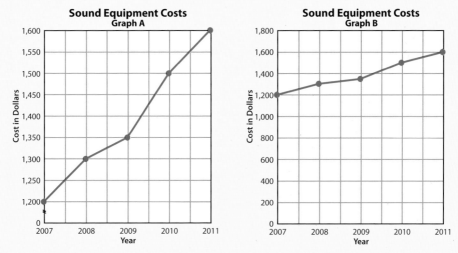

a. What was the cost of equipment each year? Does it matter which line graph you use? Why or why not?

b. Why do the two graphs look so different when they represent the same information?

Many people are excited about going to tonight's event. Yet that was not true a few weeks ago. People around town were not even aware of the concert. The event planner realized that she needed to get the word out. She had to **promote** this fundraiser.

Concert organizers promote shows in many different ways. Flyers and signs can work well. Placing them in high-traffic locations ensures that people see them. When people heard the details about the Battle of the Bands benefit, they were happy to help. They wanted to attend to show their support.

A **bar graph** is a graph that displays quantities using vertical or horizontal bars. It has a title and horizontal and vertical **axes**, which are labeled. A **scale** is used to show the **frequency** of the data. The scale runs along the side or bottom of the graph, depending on the direction of the bars.

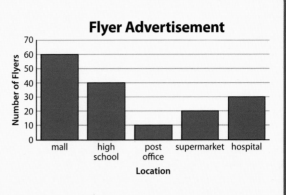

LET'S EXPLORE MATH

The event planner wanted to post flyers at local businesses. Students volunteered to help. She used a **line plot** to organize the number of businesses each student contacted. A line plot, also known as a dot plot, is a number-line diagram that uses an *x* or other mark to show the frequencies of items or categories being tallied.

Number of Businesses Contacted by Each Student

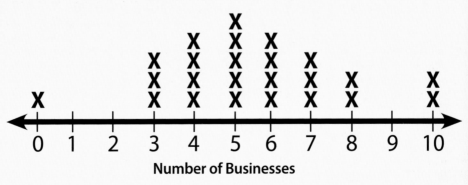

a. What does each *x* represent?

b. What do the numbers along the horizontal axis represent?

Flyers and signs were put up around town. The signs caused an immediate reaction. People started talking about the concert. They began finding friends who wanted to attend, too. They made plans for how to get there. Word-of-mouth is really important for an event like this.

Advertising an Act

Promoters can **publicize** (PUHB-luh-sahyz) musical acts in many different ways. They can use the media, like radio and television, to promote musicians through interviews. Promoters may also use a website or a social networking page to make an artist's music available online.

The local radio station has also helped promote the event. It has been running short commercials all week. These ads remind people about the important details of the event. They provide the time, location, and ticket price. The station even donated the airtime. Advertising on the radio can be expensive, but it can mean a lot more money for the cause!

Show Time!

A lot of work has been done to get ready for tonight. Now there is a lot of activity around the amphitheater. Bands are doing soundchecks. The event planner is double-checking the schedule.

amphitheater

The lighting technician is watching rehearsals. He will match the lighting to each band's performance. This concert will go into the evening. Lights will be needed to see what is happening onstage.

The concession (kuhn-SESH-uhn) stands are stocked and ready for customers. Many businesses have donated food and drink products. That means more money for tornado victims.

Concession Stands

Concession stands are big business! They bring in millions of dollars on large concert tours. People buy a lot of food and drinks when they go to a show.

Each band performs two songs. There are four judges who listen to the entire concert. After each band performs, the judges give the band a rating based on applause. The band with the highest rating at the end is the winner. There is no special prize for first place. All the musicians are really here to put on a good show and help out a good cause.

Nearly There plays for the packed amphitheater.

The crowd goes wild when the first band takes the stage! As the concert proceeds, it becomes hard to tell which band has more fans. The audience is very supportive of all the entertainers. The crowd is filled with many people who lost their homes or businesses to the tornado. The victims are grateful for everyone's support.

LET'S EXPLORE MATH

At Battle of the Bands concerts in other cities over the past few years, the winner was decided by the loudness of applause as measured in **decibels** (DES-uh-belz). Applause for one band, Sky Monkeys, was measured at four different concerts as 120 decibels, 96 decibels, 80 decibels, and 72 decibels, in that order.

a. Make a line graph that shows the applause rating in decibels for the four appearances of Sky Monkeys.

b. Describe the trend of applause for the Sky Monkeys at the four shows.

we have a winner! A band named Applesauce has been given a trophy after the judges agreed they received the loudest applause. All of the bands come out on stage for one **encore**. They dedicate the song to all the tornado victims. It is an ending that no one will ever forget!

After the show is over, the fans all leave safely and calmly. The show was a success. The event planner and other workers still have a lot of work to do. There is trash to clean up, equipment to be packed, and lights to be removed. The refreshment and souvenir stands are taken down. The amphitheater goes back to the way it was before the show. It is a long night for those people who work behind the scenes.

The Road Crew

At a large venue, there are many different people who work behind the scenes before and during a show. Those professionals are all part of the road crew. Sometimes they are called *roadies*. They travel with a band from city to city.

A Successful Event

The concert was clearly a success. The audience had a wonderful time. The bands were all enthusiastic about their performances. It was a great way for our community to help another community in need.

Another measure of the event's success was the amount of money raised. The event planner helped determine the **profit** from the concert. She had to consider how much money was spent on the event. Those costs are called **expenses**. Because of the business donations and the free performances, the expenses were much lower than they are for most concerts. The tornado victims' fund will be very pleased with this donation!

PAY TO THE ORDER OF _Tornado Victims_

Seven Thousand Five Hundred

Sept. 8 20 11

1001

09-765/432

$ 7,500.00

— DOLLARS

MEMO _____

⑈1234567891⑈ 0987654321⑈ 1001⑈

Battle of the Bands

After the Battle of the Bands was over, the organizers evaluated the profit. They looked at the **circle graph** and the bar graph below.
Use each graph to answer the questions. You may get slightly different answers from each graph.

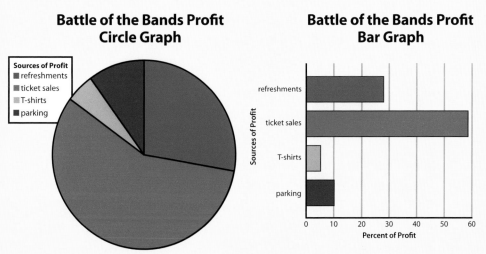

**Battle of the Bands Profit
Circle Graph**

Sources of Profit
■ refreshments
■ ticket sales
□ T-shirts
■ parking

**Battle of the Bands Profit
Bar Graph**

Sources of Profit

refreshments
ticket sales
T-shirts
parking

0 10 20 30 40 50 60
Percent of Profit

a. Name two sources of profit where one is about twice the other.

b. Name two sources of profit where one is about one-third of the other.

c. Which graph is more useful for a quick impression of how the profits are divided up?

d. Which graph is more useful for estimating the percent earned per category?

e. What scale is used on the bar graph for percent of profit?

f. If you were the organizer, how might you increase the profits for next year based on the results of the data?

The Battle of the Bands was a wonderful event. Everyone involved had one goal—to raise money for people who really need it. That would not have been possible without a lot of effort. There were many generous people who donated time, energy, and talent. Businesses worked together to donate goods and to help with concert arrangements. Finally, the bands and musicians gave a free performance. And they had a great time doing it.

No one really cared about winning the title. Everyone was a winner. The looks on the faces of the tornado victims who were helped was the real prize!

guitar technician

V.I.P. PASS
All Access

sound technician

The Tour Manager's Assistant

The band Lucky Ducky has just closed a show and is heading for the next stop on its concert tour. Lucky Ducky's tour manager needs to order items for the souvenir stands at future shows and wants to review the sales from past concerts. You are her assistant and need to present the data to her. The table below shows the number of each item sold from the past five cities on the tour.

Souvenir	Number Sold
hat	405
T-shirt	1,150
sweatshirt	960
beach towel	315
bracelet	1,570
CD	695
DVD	285

Solve It!

a. What type of graph would you create to show how many of each type of souvenir was sold? Why?

b. Create a graph to show to the tour manager that would best display the data.

c. The tour manager loves line plots and wants you to make a line plot to show how many of each type of souvenir was sold. Write an explanation to tell him why a line plot would not be the best way to display this data.

Use the steps below to help you answer the questions.

Step 1: Choose a graph (histogram, line graph, line plot, bar graph, circle graph) that would best show the data for souvenir sales.

Step 2: Create the graph. Remember to give the graph a title and label the axes (if applicable).

Step 3: Think about the number of marks you would have to make to show the number of bracelets that were sold. Write a paragraph that explains why a line plot is not the best graph for this set of data.

Glossary

amphitheater—a large, sometimes open-air building where public performances or events take place

amplify—to make a sound become louder

axes—horizontal or vertical lines from which distances are measured on a coordinate grid

bar graph—a graph in which quantities are represented by bars

circle graph—a graph that displays data as sections of a circle (also known as a pie chart)

coordinate—to organize details or events in which numerous people are involved

decibels—units of measure for the intensity (loudness) of sound

diverse—different

encore—an additional or repeated performance in response to audience demand

frequency—the number of times something occurs

histogram—a bar graph that represents the frequency of data within a data set using adjacent bars

interval—the distance between numbers from one grid line to another on a graph

line graphs—graphs that show change over time

line plot—a number line diagram that uses an x or other mark to show the frequencies of items or categories being tallied (also known as a dot plot)

profit—the money made from an activity; the amount of money left over from money received after all the costs are paid

promote—to make people aware through advertising

publicize—to provide information about a product or event so that people will know about it

scale—a system of marks at fixed intervals on a graph that are labeled with numbers

venue—a place where events, such as concerts, are held

Index

advertising, 15–17

amphitheater, 8, 11, 18, 20, 22

bar graph, 15, 25, 29

benefit concerts, 5–6, 14

booking agent, 10

circle graph, 25, 29

decibels, 21

dot plot, 15

event planner, 7–11, 14–15, 18, 22, 24

histogram, 7, 9, 11, 29

lighting technician, 19

line graph, 13, 29

line plot, 15, 29

road crew (roadies), 23

scale, 15

sound technician, 12, 27

stage manager, 8–10, 12

word-of-mouth, 16

Let's Explore Math

Page 7:

a. 10 songs

b. 0 people

c. Answers will vary but may include: around 20 songs; The majority of the people surveyed said they would prefer 20–29 songs, but many people also said they would prefer 10–19 songs.

Page 9:

a. 5 songs

b. 20–24 songs

Page 11:

a. Maximum: 168 minutes; Minimum: 75 minutes

b. One possible answer: 20 minutes

c. One possible answer:

d. 120–139 minutes

Page 13:

a. 2007: $1,200; 2008: $1,300; 2009: $1,350; 2010: $1,500; 2011: $1,600. No; The graphs display the same information.

Page 13 *(cont.)*:

b. The graphs look different because the interval (scale) is different for the cost in dollars.

Page 15:

a. 1 student

b. The horizontal axis numbers represent the number of businesses contacted by each student.

Page 21:

a.

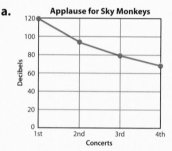

b. The amount of applause the Sky Monkeys received decreased over time.

Page 25:

a. parking and T-shirts, or refreshments and ticket sales

b. parking and refreshments

c. circle graph

d. bar graph

e. 10%

f. Answers will vary.

Problem-Solving Activity

a. A bar graph is the best way to display the large numbers of souvenirs sold because you can adjust the frequency interval to make a manageable graph.

b.

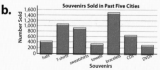

c. Answers should address the fact that line plots are not the best graph to display this data because the number of marks needed would be far too great.